THE BIBLE IN THE CHURCH AND KINGDOM

In the Beginning was the Word ...

Churches have not always housed large books called Bibles. This only became common in the 16th century with the invention of the printing press. But without the contents of the Bible, the library of writings it contains, the Church might have died in infancy. These 'books' tell of how God speaks and acts to create and redeem his world, and of how all the unmet promises of God will finally be fulfilled. The climax of this revelation is the person of Jesus Christ, who comes into the world to make God fully known to his people. As St John says at the beginning of his Gospel, 'In the beginning was the Word ... and the Word became flesh and dwelt among us'.

The Anglo-Saxon clergy who led the first Winchester Cathedral, the building now called Old Minster, needed these Holy Scriptures as much as any other. From its foundation in the mid-7th century, the Cathedral continued to grow and develop for the next 400 years before the Norman Conquest. In these years of relative wealth and stability the Cathedral's need for copies of the Scriptures, books of prayers and music for worship, and many other goods for the life of the community, resulted in a rich tradition of literature, art and craftsmanship.

In 961 Bishop Æthelwold replaced the secular clerks running Old Minster with Benedictine monks from his monastery in Abingdon, Oxfordshire, and with Archbishop Dunstan of Canterbury and King Edgar standardised monastic practice over the kingdom using the Rule of St Benedict. Benedict had understood the need for the monks to draw deeply from the Holy Scriptures. He legislated for them to be heard and used in worship eight times daily, and at mealtimes. For Benedict, obeying the Word of God offered in the Scriptures and through the counsel of monastic superiors was the surest way to salvation:

Listen carefully, my child, to the Master's instructions and attend to them with the ear of your heart ... As we progress in this way of life and in faith we shall run on the path of God's commandments, our hearts overflowing with the inexpressible delight of love. (Prologue)

Front cover: f.270v Song of Songs, *Leaping Figures Master. Inside flap:* f.210 Prologue and Book of Haggai, *Genesis Initial Master over design of Apocrypha Drawings Master. Inside front cover:* From Æthelwold's Book of Blessings, c.970–80 – pre-Conquest art of the 'Winchester School' © The British Library Board / Add. 49598, f.45v.

The Bible provided not only a way of life and prayer for the monastic community, it described the way the world was and how everyone in society was called to live under God's rule: kings, nobles, knights, merchants and peasants all had their place. In the Middle Ages the Church had the power to be able to work towards this vision throughout the territories of the former Roman Empire. The monks were expected to live exemplary lives of faith within a society governed by God through the Church, His authorised agency. At the top of this hierarchy there was a balance of power to be maintained under God between the Church's leaders, the bishops, and the anointed head of society, the king.

Two of Bishop Henry's benefactions in Winchester: an almshouse at St Cross; a font at the Cathedral.

The Power of the Bible

In the 1990s the then Prime Minister of Great Britain was strongly advised that politicians 'don't do God'. In the 12th century, however, when the Winchester Bible was commissioned, a division between the sacred and the secular would have been impossible even to imagine. The Bible's likely sponsor, Henry of Blois, typified this mix: grandson of William the Conqueror, the first Norman king of England; but also raised and educated in the magnificent Abbey of Cluny in France, where he was professed a monk.

Like St Swithun's Priory, the Abbey of Cluny followed the Rule of St Benedict, in a version that placed emphasis on the care of the poor and the richness of worship. Many of the aristocracy were groomed there for high office. It is not surprising that someone formed in this tradition both founded an almshouse in Winchester, The Hospital of St Cross, and amassed for his Priory Church a large collection of treasures, including a Tournai marble font still used in baptism in the Cathedral today.

A man of Henry's position was bound to be both a man of God and player in the political struggles of his day, including the long civil war ending in 1153 between his brother King Stephen and the Empress Matilda, daughter of Henry I. Unfortunately Henry had ended up on the wrong side, which resulted in his leaving England for a period of self-imposed exile and travelling around Europe.

His travels took him back to Cluny and also to Rome, where he may have seen the magnificent 9th-century French Bible given to Pope John III in 875, probably the inspiration for the giant Bibles promoted by the papacy across Europe from around 1070. Henry was a lover of books, which in the 12th century were rare and precious commodities written and crafted entirely by hand.

After his pardon by King Stephen's successor, Henry II, Henry of Blois returned to Winchester in 1158 and set about securing his position by ensuring that the Priory of St Swithun returned to its pre-eminence in the kingdom. A strong monastery reflected well on the king whose sacred duty included supporting the Church. In turn the Church benefited his rule by reinforcing social stability and praying for the soul of its patron. A strong Church meant strong support in uncertain times.

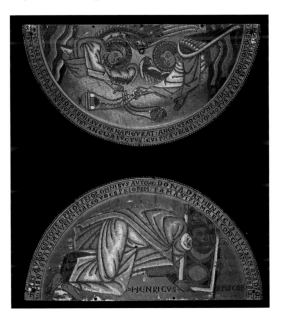

Two plaques, c.1150–70, the lower showing Henry in the traditional pose of a donor © The Trustees of the British Museum.

Henry of Blois (1098?–1171) was a man who made enemies. Bernard of Clairvaux, leader of the reforming Cistercian movement, fell out with him when Henry secured the post of Archbishop of York for one of his nephews. No insult was spared for 'the old warlock of Winchester' and 'the whore who sits for sale by the wayside, soliciting all who pass by'! Another critic called him 'a new kind of monster made up of opposites, part monk, part soldier'.

Yet Henry was capable of great acts of generosity, such as underwriting all expenses at the Abbey of Cluny for an entire year whilst repairing their financial administration. His genius for administration led to his pardon, even though King Henry II knew that Bishop Henry was a character unlikely to be tamed even in his old age. In fact, the last public act that the Bishop performed just days before his death was to rebuke the king for prompting the murder of Archbishop Thomas Becket.

Bishop Henry rapidly made his mark. Before his exile he had re-modelled the east end of the Cathedral Choir to give pilgrims closer access to the relics of St Swithun. Now he placed the bones of bishops and pre-Conquest kings in the closest proximity to them, stressing the continuities between the Saxon and Norman orders. Henry began his great Bible, drawing on the pre-Conquest tradition of Winchester as a seat of learning but open to the new Byzantine style coming from the east of the Roman Empire. Like the holy relics housed in the Cathedral, this was to be an object that communicated the power of God and proved the prestige of Bishop Henry's priory.

Honesty compels us to admit that there is no conclusive evidence that Bishop Henry commissioned this Bible. However, the earlier English giant Bibles were all commissioned by either kings or bishops, such as the one brought over from Normandy by Bishop Carilef of Durham or the one sponsored by King Stephen, now called the Lambeth Bible but probably gifted to his royal abbey and mausoleum at Faversham in Kent. Bishop Henry himself had previously commissioned two great Bibles, one for his Abbey at Glastonbury where he had been and continued as abbot, and the other, not yet finished, for the Priory at Winchester itself.

Bishop Henry's new Bible was clearly intended to surpass in splendour all previous efforts – the ones he had seen in exile, the ones now being produced in the other great monasteries of England, such as in Bury St Edmunds in Suffolk, and even the one commissioned by him for Winchester before his exile (now housed in the Bodleian Library, Oxford, England). This new Bible's height and width were limited by the maximum size parchment could be – every usable inch of a calf's skin, from neck to sternum, from spine to the belly flanks. The immensity of the object would engender awe and wonder. But in addition to this, the space allowed plenty of room around the text, and illustrations in miniature left even greater scope for a huge amount of detail and variety to be fitted into these spaces.

The sheer ambition of this project is hard to grasp. The fact that work stopped on the Bible around the time of Bishop Henry's death shows how completely dependent the Priory was on his drive and financial backing. A Bible of this scale would have cost its patron about as much as a small castle. The illustrations of the Hebrew Scriptures were sumptuous enough, but the ones planned for the New Testament were bound to exceed them in every way.

The Morgan Leaf, now kept in the Morgan Library in New York, gives an indication of the direction of travel. This single leaf was not planned in the original scheme of the Bible, but hooked into the standard binding just before 1 Samuel. This book already included a fine initial based on the events of the first chapter. However, the Morgan Leaf covers a wider span, the careers of Samuel the prophet and King David recounted over the next two books. Samuel was the son of Hannah, whose lament over her childlessness and her thanks to God after his birth are portrayed in the following initial. The Leaf and the initial tie closely together narratively as well as stylistically.

With this leaf and others designed but unfinished, the one standing as a preface to the Book of Judith and the one facing the Book of Maccabees, it would surely have provided an impetus, had Bishop Henry lived, for other single leaves to be introduced at highpoints in the narrative, such as at the start of the four Gospels or Apocalypse. Matthew's Gospel as it now stands, for example, begins with a very meagre initial, but the three preceding leaves are now missing.

Left: f.88 1 Samuel, *Morgan Leaf Master over design of Apocrypha Drawings Master. Opposite:* Morgan Leaf verso, *Morgan Leaf Master over design of Apocrypha Drawings Master* © 2014. Photo Pierpont Morgan Library/Art Resource/ Scala, Florence.

Historiated initials are enlarged and decorated initial letters that tell a story. They started to be used in the British Isles in manuscripts of the 8th century and came about through the fusion of Irish and Saxon styles. One of the tiny points of detail that re-emerged in the conservation was the silk thread sewn into the parchment near some of these initials. These were used to attach silk curtains to the parchment so that they could be covered over. They were not very practical as it made shutting the Bible with the curtains in place difficult. They may have helped to prevent abrasion by the facing leaf, but they certainly would have enhanced the drama of the text, adding another, physical way by which the mystery of the Scripture would gradually be revealed.

Text and Image Together

While the text is easily overlooked today as the backdrop for the illustrated initials, both were treated with the same amount of care and seen as a unity. The difference was that the expertise to write the text probably resided in the Priory. The monastic Rule encouraged both manual work and the close study of the Scriptures: these two callings were gloriously combined in the role of the scribe, who in his work could meditate on the text sentence by sentence, word by word, letter by letter. A scribe was usually exempted from other forms of monastic work to concentrate on this sacred work.

The monastery might contain many scribes, but Winchester's text shows that just one was entrusted with the ordinary text of this Bible, someone with an old-fashioned hand even for his day – no doubt the most senior. The evenness of his hand not only bears tribute to his manual dexterity but also demonstrates the quality of his steady, contemplative attention as he set about his task.

Before the writing began the scribe, or an assistant, had to prick and rule the text. First the frame for the text was set out; wide margins were a luxury only afforded to the most expensive texts. Then, to maintain uniformity across leaves, the line spacing was established by pricking with a point of a knife through the gatherings of the manuscript. These marks were sometimes trimmed away at the binding, but can still be seen in the Winchester Bible. Finally, the lines were ruled with the back of the knife or a stylus.

Certainly the scribe made errors, which would usually be scraped out as he went along. Sometimes mistakes would be picked up later by an editor. The biggest correction in the whole manuscript is at the beginning of Isaiah, where an entire two-leaf spread had to be replaced, probably because of an irretrievable error. The editor duly supplied this in a darker ink and a later hand, but trying to imitate the original scribe's.

One page of this Bible was about a day's work, and there were a thousand pages to write in all. It is this monk who left instructions in the margins for the more specialist rubricators who would add the display lettering in red, blue and green ink. (In the Bible there are

Top: f.204 Prologue to Jonah, *Genesis Initial Master.*
Above: Section of text showing accents added for reading aloud as well as editorial correction.
Opposite: f.109 1 Kings, *Amalekite Master over design by Leaping Figures Master.*

T.
REX.
DD.
SE
NV
ERAT.

habebatq; etatis plurimos dies · Cumq; opi
retur uestibus · non calefiebat · Dixerunt g
serui sui · Queramus dno nro regi   adolescen
tulam uirginem · & stet coram rege & foueat
eum · dormiatq; in sinu suo · & calefaciat dnm
nrm regem · Quesierunt igitur adolescentulam
speciosam in omnib; finibus isrl · & inuenerunt
abisag sunamiten · & adduxerunt eam ad regem ·
Erat aute puella pulchra nimis · dormiebatq;
cum rege · & ministrabat ei · Rex uero non cogno
uit eam · Adonias aute filius agith · eleuabat
dicens · Ego regnabo · Fecitq; sibi currus & equi
tes · & quinquaginta uiros qui ante eum curre
rent · nec corripuit eum pater suus aliquando
dicens · Quare hoc fecisti? Erat autem & ipse
pulcher ualde · secundus natu post absalon ·

two distinct styles of rubrication, the square and rounded.) This monk had also to leave sufficient space for the illumination and the display lettering which began the first initial and line of each book of the Bible. The slowing of the eye achieved by these devices was a sign to treat the whole text following as sacred, by attending to the beauty and richness pregnant in each and every word.

The text had to be as accurate as possible to the European standard. Great Bibles were the result of Archbishop Lanfranc's drive to standardise the Church's sacred text. This was achieved by having a text to copy from and check against in the monastery. The version used was the Vulgate, a Latin translation derived from St Jerome in the 4th century AD. Jerome was the first scholar to go back to the Hebrew of the Old Testament, rather than translating into Latin from the Greek version of the Septuagint, a translation of the Old Testament created for Greek-speaking Jews in the 2nd century before Christ.

The monks thought that an accurate text was itself a wonder. Though a contemporary viewer puzzles over an editor leaving corrections in the margins rather than hiding them away in the gutter or scraping them off, the truth is that these refinements were welcomed as part of the scenery of the sacred text, just as the accents added to help monks read aloud or the careful attention to punctuation or the illuminations. All these encouraged the Scriptures to be read, marked, learnt and inwardly digested.

Left: f.1 St Jerome's Letter to Paulinus, *Genesis Initial Master* – the saint at his writing desk. *Opposite:* f.69 Book of Joshua, *Amalekite Master over design by Leaping Figures Master* – contemporary armour.

It is possible that the scribe writing the Bible was not a Priory monk but a lay professional. They are documented as being employed in writing books at Abingdon Abbey, for example, in the early 12th century, and later at St Albans. All we know is that Bishop Henry would have wanted to secure the service of the most skilled available craftsmen, and that if he had to pay for this, then that would not have been a deterrent. However, unlike for the Bury Bible, a single lay artist was not in charge of the project from the outset, rather the artists fitted in with what the scribe had already done. It also seems reasonable to suppose that Winchester's Scriptorium retained real expertise, not only a rich tradition of manuscript production, which might have been up to even this great task. Whichever it was, a lay scribe as much as a monk could become totally absorbed in his task, to which the wonderfully even writing testifies.

T.
F.
A.
C.
TV.
C.

VT. POST. MORE. MOYSI.

The monks' awareness of the need for careful interpretation of the Scriptures is established from the outset in the Winchester Bible. Before the first book, Genesis, a letter is included from St Jerome himself to Paulinus, Bishop of Nola, encouraging him to study the Scriptures diligently to attain wisdom and insight. As he says of the passages he cites in that letter, 'these references convey one meaning upon the surface, but another below it'.

This is immediately followed by another of Jerome's letters, to 'Desiderius'. It defends his new translation of the Pentateuch, the first five books of the Bible, against detractors. In the process Jerome reveals that this 'dearest Desiderius' is the one who commissioned the work. This makes the name – not that of any Pope in Jerome's time or after – a playful variant on Damasus, the Pope 'desirous' of a fresh translation.

The message of the initial D of the prologue to the books that follow is clear: Jerome passes his translation not to Pope 'Desiderius' but to Bishop Henry, standing in his full pontifical robes with his freshly published Bible under his arm next to his crosier, both marking his authority as a Church leader (see p.29). A closer and more flattering association with the Pope could not have been possible, and one echoing Henry's tireless efforts to secure the role of papal legate (ambassador) in England.

As this example illustrates, the illuminated initials had multiple functions within the text. They enhanced its appearance and underlined its value; they enhanced the status of its patron; they helped monks to navigate through the text and to remember key events and themes in each book; and most crucially they helped monks to interpret the text. For example, the soldiers' armour and the military architecture were contemporary, meaning that the stories were for their own time.

Top: f.169 Book of Baruch, *Morgan Leaf Master* – contemporary architecture. *Below:* f.170v Prologue to Ezekiel, *Morgan Leaf Master* – Christ's Passion prefigured. *Opposite:* f.200v Book of Joel, *Apocrypha Drawings Master* – the Holy Spirit empowers Joel's preaching.

Another important way in which the illumination helped interpretation, as commended by Jerome, was the reading of the Old Testament in the light of Jesus Christ, who came to fulfil the promises of the Law and the Prophets and embodied the Wisdom and Spirit of God. For example, the initial at the start of the book of Numbers comes, unusually, from a scene from the middle of the book, and shows Moses holding up the fiery serpent on a pole to save the people from death. It is used because it foreshadows Jesus being lifted up on the cross for the salvation of the world (cf. Jn 3.14–15). Likewise, the prophet Ezekiel being led into captivity resembles a scene from Christ's Passion and the prophet Joel preaching that the Lord will come summons a dove, the sign of the Holy Spirit.

di in uulnur meum: & iuuene in liuoze meu.
Et esaias. Audite celi & auribus pape terra.

INCIPIT IOhEL PROPhETA:

ERBV

DOMINI

QVOD

FACTVM EST AD IOhEL FILIVM BAThVEL. Aud

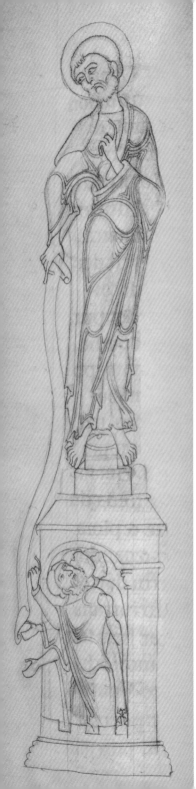

How the Images Were Made

The Winchester Bible, being unfinished, gives an unrivalled opportunity to study the making of its images. Every stage of the process is represented. It starts with the scribe leaving space for the image, with a marginal note about the letter or scene required, although sometimes this wasn't obeyed. As the artists were not always on site, the precise dimensions must sometimes have relied on the scribe's judgement and practical imagination. As a result, the artist occasionally has more to say than can be fitted in without compromising the text or insufficient inspiration to fill it.

The first contribution of the artist was to sketch the picture with a lead stylus known as a plummet. The design was then worked up precisely in ink and plummet, to avoid the lead granules showing through the final design. This was followed by the gilding, with fine gold and silver leaf laid on a platform of gesso (layers of binder and chalk) and then burnished with a tooth or polished stone. The paint was then applied in layers to the ungilded areas, sometimes by different artists, with the fine details in the drapery and faces being completed last of all.

In the later parts of the manuscript the collaboration between scribe and artist becomes tighter. The Master of the Leaping Figures does all the underdrawing and sometimes works in a space where, unusually, the display lettering has already been finished. Does this suggest that in the later stages of the project one artist took over the burden of the work and, having ample employment, stayed in the Priory as a resident artist?

The artist was responsible for grinding and mixing all the pigments and adding binder – egg yolk and gum arabic – to form the paints. Medieval pigments came from a variety of natural sources: animal, vegetable and mineral. Far more valuable than gold was the pigment ultramarine, made from the mineral lapis lazuli, which came only from Afghanistan. The explorer Marco Polo only reached the mines in 1271, exactly one hundred years after Bishop Henry's death and the premature end of the Winchester Bible project.

Opposite, left: cf.429 Epistle of James, Leaping Figures Master – drawn only.
Opposite, right: f.268 Ecclesiastes, Leaping Figures Master – drawn and gilded.
Below: f.246 Psalm 101, Morgan Leaf Master over design by Leaping Figures Master – drawn, gilded and partially painted.

THE ARTISTS OF THE WINCHESTER BIBLE

The foremost authority on the Winchester Bible in the 20th century, Walter Oakeshott, Honorary Librarian of the Cathedral and Headmaster of Winchester College, detected six different artistic styles in the illuminations of the Bible. His theory that each style was the work of one 'master' and his apprentices has held sway since the 1940s.

Pre-eminent is the Master of the Leaping Figures. He is responsible for much of the underdrawing and becomes the dominant artist as the project progresses. He is the most dramatic of the artists, responsible for the sinuous figures and their dampfold clothing – which one modern commentator has dubbed 'the wet T-shirt look'! However, the work of at least five other master artists is evident. The Master of the Genesis Initial often portrays robust figures with intense, frowning faces, employing a strong palette of red and blue. The Amalekite Master offers soft drapery and lax limbs. The Master of the Morgan Leaf paints solemn figures and includes twining decorative stems bearing leaves of many colours. The Master of the Gothic Majesty, probably the least experienced of the artists, fails to convey much emotion. The Master of the Apocrypha Drawings contributes the design of the major leaves, filling the spaces with elegant, overlapping figures and using a lighter palette which includes pink, pale blue and yellow.

While the genius of their work can only be considered at depth in a few instances, most are illustrated in the pages of this guide. However, it is easy to see at a glance the way in which even the same subject, in this case a man wrestling with a lion, is treated entirely differently by the different master.

Top: f.131 Book of Isaiah, *Gothic Majesty Master.*
Above, left: f.201v Book of Amos, *Morgan Leaf Master over design by Leaping Figures Master.*
Above, right: f.205 Book of Micah, *Genesis Initial Master over design by Apocrypha Drawings Master.*

The Master of the Leaping Figures
EXODUS INITIAL

The Book of Exodus begins with the initial H of Haec, meaning 'These': 'These are the names of the sons of Israel'. Exodus is a story of the liberation of the Hebrew people from slavery, so it is fitting that the oppression is represented at the very start, with the Egyptian taskmaster poking at the eye of the Hebrew slave and grasping him roughly round the arm. The conflict is heightened by a tangle of arms and legs on the central vertical and the opposed background decoration on either side.

The composition of the lower part of the initial is altogether different and built on a diagonal starting from the bottom left-hand corner. Again the figure on the left – the dominant side from which we read – has the upper hand. This time it is Moses, raised in the Egyptian court but born a Hebrew, whose gesture outreaches and outmatches that of the assailant above.

By multiple means the artist conveys a mighty blow that brings justice – the angle of the staff at its point of greatest momentum, the naked calves flexed, the knees bent, the cape and garment flowing behind as the whole body drives forward, and the background decoration pressing down on the weapon.

The Egyptian begins to collapse while remaining vertical so as not to disturb the composition overall. Beneath him lies a small pile of sand, signifying that Moses will attempt to hide the body by burying him.

cf.21v Book of Exodus, *Leaping Figures Master.*

It is hard to imagine a better used initial. Even the middle bar of the letter provides both a mound for battle above and a way of giving Moses some headroom beneath, in marked contrast to his victim. It is not surprising that the artist took every inch of space available for the illustration, not even leaving room for the first, rubricated line of the text.

BOOK OF PSALMS, PSALM 1

Another initial employing strong contrasts and drawn by the Master of the Leaping Figures is the introduction to the Book of Psalms. This book in the Bible is unique in that each psalm is offered in two versions, in parallel columns. This is a reflection of their importance as the mainstay of prayer in monastic worship. Psalms provided the monks with words to offer adoration, praise, thanksgiving and lament to God.

The first psalm begins with a B for Beatus: 'Blessed is the man who has not walked in the counsel of the ungodly'. It is about choosing a godly path and avoiding a life rooted in wickedness that cannot endure. The contrast between these two foundations for living, eternal or ephemeral, is highlighted here.

The author of the Psalms was thought to be King David. David first came to prominence when the Israelites were challenged by the Philistines to take on their giant soldier Goliath. No one would, except for the shepherd-boy David, who proved his credentials and intentions by telling King Saul of Israel of his power to guard the flock. Any bears and lions daring to take off sheep had been pursued and clubbed or, if they had dared to turn and fight, had had the lamb torn from their jaw. Such would be the fate of Goliath (1 Sam. 17.34ff). Note that the deliverance in the bottom loop of the left-hand B, from jaw rather than paw, is the greater.

While all this is beautifully depicted, the designer has more to show than natural deliverance: Jesus Christ, a shepherd-king greater than even King David, protects his flock from evil. The B on the right, therefore, depicts two scenes of Jesus rescuing his own people and once again the one in the lower loop is the greater. In the top loop Christ performs an exorcism (Mk 9.14ff) and in the bottom loop Christ harrows hell, descending into the Devil's own lair, with the thief whom he has just pardoned on the cross at his side, to release those trapped in the very jaw of death. Note the eye of the abyss – a monstrous beast, worse than any lion. In this the greatest deliverance of all, the last bastion of evil is uprooted.

Further contrasts accentuate the message that Christ's deliverance is definitive. The large bear confronting David looks fairly shocked, but the demon expelled at the exorcism is puny and terrified. The lion turning around has the temerity to look David in the eye, while the prostrate Devil averts his gaze and quakes. Though his hands are bound, he tries somehow to protect himself from being trampled. Christ's power over evil is stressed by the extreme angle of his head and the lunge of his body and shepherd's staff, bearing down on evil. This also has the merit of allowing this towering figure to fit into the available space.

Opposite: f.218 Psalm 1, *Genesis Initial Master over design by Leaping Figures Master.*
Below: f.169 Prayer of Jeremiah, *Morgan Leaf Master.*

Sed in lege dñi uoluntaf ei· & in lege ciuf medita
bitur die ac nocte·   T'pore suo·
Et erit tanquã lignũ quod plantatũ est secus

Sed in lege dñi uoluntas eius· & in lege eius
tabitur die ac nocte·   T'pore suo·
Et erit tanquã lignũ transplantatum iuxta
le aquarum· quod fructum suum dabit

One final feature worth noting is the emphasis on mouths. The Psalms were meant to be recited by heart. Novices were given extra time in the day to learn them. The monks who used them in worship and called them to mind as they undertook manual work thought of them as a way of purifying their hearts and rooting their lives in righteousness. Worship began with the response, 'O Lord, open our lips; and our mouth shall proclaim your praise'. It was fitting that the mouth should feature so prominently as a key monastic concern at the start of this book.

THE CALL OF THE PROPHET JEREMIAH, AND ELIJAH'S DENUNCIATION, 2 KINGS

The Master of the Leaping Figures also paints two particularly powerful initials in the books of the prophets. At the start of Jeremiah, he portrays not only the obvious shock and hesitation of the prophet in the recoiling figure, as God touches him on the mouth to speak his words; he also portrays Jeremiah's desire to serve God, as he stands on tip-toe to meet him. His looking into the eyes of God beautifully captures both trust and ambivalence. The budding almond trees around the prophet refer to a pun in the text on the Hebrew words for 'almond' and 'watching'. God will watch over Jeremiah as he speaks for Him, so he should not fear.

Fear works in the other direction in the initial beginning 2 Kings. The prophet points an accusing finger at King Ahaziah, who dared to consult foreign gods about his illness. The illuminated edges of their cloaks – Elijah's pointed and the king's shaped like a gigantic ear – highlight who is commissioned to speak and who must listen. The power of Elijah's word is cleverly backed up by luxuriant vegetation sprouting about him and the supporting heavenly chariot, from a later scene in the story where he is translated into heaven. As he returns to heaven, his cloak falls back to earth to give his successor Elisha 'a double measure' of his spirit. The artist has managed to squeeze in the horses but is unable to work with the space left in the text for the cloak. Its turning from gold to blue on its descent is a nice touch, allowing strong contrasts with the background both inside and outside the initial.

Left: f.120v 2 Kings, *Leaping Figures Master.*
Opposite: f.148 Book of Jeremiah, *Leaping Figures Master.*

INCIPIT LIBER IEREMIE PROPHETE:

V

E
R
B
A.

I
E
R
E

M I E.

The Master of the Genesis Initial

The initials at Psalm 1 designed by the Master of the Leaping Figures were, according to Oakeshott, painted by the Master of the Genesis Initial. It is this master whose work illustrates the very start of the Bible and shows conclusively how the Hebrew Scriptures were read by Christian interpreters, as part of a story of promise and fulfilment.

The Genesis Initial is the capital I beginning 'In principio', 'In the beginning'. It begins with a birth, the joyous entry of Eve into the world, made by God out of a rib from the sleeping Adam, the man of the earth. God greets her warmly. This is not the Eve who later tempts her male companion to disobey God, but the one whose creation makes possible the human family and therefore the birth of Jesus Christ.

The 'fall' of humankind is represented in the next medallion, in the bodies drowned in the flood, floating in the waters beneath Noah's ark. But the emphasis is on the dove returning to the ark (depicted here as the Church, the Ark of Salvation) in whose beak is held a freshly plucked olive leaf, a sign of the waters' subsiding and God's promise of deliverance from the deluge honoured.

This promise of deliverance is tested again in the next medallion: Abram is offering his only son and heir to God in sacrifice; but the angel stays his hand and provides instead a ram caught in a thicket. His willingness to sacrifice Isaac prefigures God's willingness to give up his beloved Son Jesus Christ. It is rewarded by another promise, that his descendants will be as numerous as the stars.

The promise is tested once again as the Israelites are forced into the wilderness and are in danger of losing their way. It is re-established by the giving of the Law. Clouds cover the summit of the holy mountain when Moses sees God face-to-face and receives the Ten Commandments. Obeying them will bring life and blessing.

Despite the dire rule of Saul, God finds another way to bring blessing to his people, this time through a king. In the fifth medallion we see the prophet Samuel anointing David, the ancestor of Jesus Christ through his father Joseph. The true king is coming.

Joseph himself appears in the medallion below with his betrothed Mary. She has just given birth to her son, who lies behind in a crib that looks like a sarcophagus, which hints at Jesus' death and resurrection. The ox and ass look on in fulfilment of the prophecy in Isaiah that these creatures would recognise their master, while both parents seem to be puzzling deeply over the meaning of the birth.

The final medallion takes up an image for the very last book of the Bible, the Revelation given to John of the time when all God's promises are finally fulfilled. The rainbow in the Noah story, which was not depicted in the second medallion, is displayed here in double measure. Christ holds a green cross signifying the defeat of death on the tree of life and the renewal of creation. In the bottom corners of the initial, under the medallion, the dead are raised from their graves, ready to enter into Christ's triumph in heaven.

f.5 Book of Genesis, *Genesis Initial Master*. A story of promise and fulfilment – the God who creates humanity in the first medallion foreshadows the Christ who redeems humanity in the last.

EXPLICIT LIB REG V. I.

INCIP CAPLA LIBRI REG II:

D e planctu dauid quomodo lxint Saul & Ionathas · I.
D e reditu dauid in hebron ubi secundo unctus est · II.
& de abner & ysbosech & Ioab · & de prelio ubi luserint pueri
& Asael occubuit · III. filii Saul ·
D e filiis dauid in hebron natis · & quomodo cepit recepit
Michol · & de Abner a Ioab interfecto · & de morte ysbosech
D e cunctis tribubus secutis dauid · & quomodo
ingressus est Syon & de hiis artificibus & lignis · & de urouib;
& filiis qui nati sunt ei · V. fuerit Nationes.
D e duobus preliis quibus ... dauid percussit philisteos ·
& de Arca adducta in Ierusalem · VI. secura ·
D e Nathan ppheta ubi phibuit dauid edificare templu
& pphetat de xpo · & quomodo dauid in uirtute humilia
D e miphibosech filio Ionathe · & de Anon rege · VII.
Amon quomodo illuserit pueri dauid & de uindicta in
D e bethsabee uxore urie parabola p nathan · VIII.
& de morte pueri de stupro nati · & de natiuitate Salomonis ·
D e urbe Rabbath ad dauid capta · & que de Ammon IX.
& thamar memorantur · & de Absalon quomodo interfec
D e fuga Absalon ad hostias · X. Amnon ·
regem syrie ingressus · & de muliere thecuite que p eo da
uid locuta est · XI. modo patri expulit regno ·
D e Absalon pulchritudine · & quot habuerit filios · & quo
D e consilio Acrofel & chusai dato Absalon · XII.
& de Achimaas & Ionathan exploratoribus dauid ·
D e bello ubi Absalon piit · & quom cum dauid lxint · XIII.
D e reditu dauid in ierlm & recuperatione regni · XIIII.
D e Siba qui cum parte populi rebellauit contra dauid XV.
& de Amasa quem interfecit Ioab · & de fame que accidit
p gabaonitas · quos ultus est dauid in septem crucifixis
de stirpe Saul · XVI. Iurantibus ·
D e prelio philistinorum in quo dauid patuit discrimini ·
& de reliquis bellis · & de Cantico · & de prophetia de xpo ·
D e uiris fortissimis ipsius Cum dauid · & de cog. XVII.
D e indignatione diuina · cur dauid populum · XVIII.
iusserit numerari · & de optione p Gad tribus modis obla
ta · & de interfectione in septuaginta milium p angelu
illata · & de sacrificio oblato ad dauid in Area Areuna re
buSet ·

EXPLICIUNT CAPLA:

INCIPIT LIBER ;

AC.

TV.

EST.

AUTEM POSTQUAM

MORTUUS EST SAUL · ut dauid re
uerteretur accede amalech & ma
neret in siceleg dies duos · In die au
tem tertia apparuit homo ueniens
de castris saul ueste conscissa · &
puluere aspersus caput · Et ut ue
nit ad dauid · cecidit sup faciem
suam & adorauit · Dixitq; ad eum
Vnde uenis? Qui ait ad eum · De
castris istl fugi · Et dixit ad eum
dauid · Quod est uerbu quod fac
tum est? In dic a michi · Qui ait ·
Fugit populus e prelio · & multi
corruentes e populo mortui sunt ·
sed & saul & ionathan filius eius
interierunt · Dixitq; dauid ad ad
olescentem · qui nuntiabat ei · Vn
de scis quia mortuus est saul & io
nathan filius eius? Ait ad olescens
qui narrabat ei · Casu ueni in mon
tem gelboe · & saul incumbebat
sup hastam suam · porro currus &
equites appropinquabant ei · Et
conuersus post tergum suum · uidens
que me uocauit · Cui cum respondis
sem assum · dixit michi · Quis nam
es tu? Et aio ad eum · Amalechites
sum · Et locutus est michi · Sta
sup me & interfice me · qm tenent
me angustie · & adhuc tota anima
mea in me est · Stansq; sup eum · occidi illum ·
Sciebam enim · quod uiuere non poterat post
ruinam · Et tuli diadema quod erat in capite
eius · & armillam de brachio illius · & attuli
ad te dnm meu huc · Apprehendens autem da
uid uestimenta sua scidit · omisq; uiri qui erant
cum eo · & planxerunt & fleuerunt & ieiuna
uerunt usq; ad uesperam · sup saul & sup iona
than filium eius · & sup populum dni & sup do
mum isrl · quod corruissent gladio · Dixitq;

The Amalekite Master, over a design by the Leaping Figures Master
2 SAMUEL

The artistry in the opening initial of 2 Samuel tells a story of justice and succession. Saul was the first anointed king of Israel, but David, his successor, was remembered as the nation's greatest king. To represent David taking over the throne from Saul, following Saul's death in battle, would be a delicate business; there had to be no sense in which David was complicit in Saul's downfall.

The role of passing over the crown fell to an unfortunate Amalekite. He was the one who, having run the dying Saul through at his own request, took the crown from his head, and a bracelet (2 Sam. 1.10). The killing is not shown. Saul is portrayed at rest, his limbs entwined with those of his beloved son Jonathan, his palm outstretched towards him. We see instead the moment when the Amalekite steals in to remove the crown. Note his placement at the very centre of the composition and the way that the shield on his back gives him and Saul a moment of privacy in the heat of battle, gloriously represented by the clatter of swords, originally gilded in silver, spilling out of the initial.

Reading down the initial we come to a splendid roof under which David is seated, as if already enthroned. The Amalekite kneels outside the initial, prominent but clearly foreign to David's camp, doing David obeisance and presenting a token of his succession, the bracelet. David rends his garments (2 Sam. 1.11), showing his remorse over Saul's death, thereby exonerating himself from any complicity in the act.

The composition makes the succession obvious. The heads of Saul and David are brought together as closely as possible: Saul with the Amalekite stooping over him and stealing the crown from him, and David with the Amalekite kneeling under him and offering him tribute, ornately crowned by a palace roof and knot-work decoration above.

The injustice of Saul's killing is stressed and redressed by the slaying of the Amalekite. The one who has dared to handle the signs of Saul's royal office dies empty-handed. The Israelite sword falling on the bottom left-hand side of the initial balances the flailing swords of the enemy on the top right-hand side. Justice is done and Saul's honour upheld by King David's own command.

Above: f.77v Book of Judges, a cut-out initial P.
Opposite: f.99v 2 Samuel, *Amalekite Master over design by Leaping Figures Master.*

THE CONSERVATION OF THE WINCHESTER BIBLE

The conservation of the Bible was meticulously planned and could only begin once a panel of experts had given its approval. The plan was to unbind each volume, fully conserve and stabilise the manuscript, and then rebind it to provide the manuscript, with the most relaxed opening possible for the benefit of future generations.

Our experts agreed that only one man could be trusted with a job of this significance: Christopher Clarkson, a book conservator of international renown who happened to be living in Oxford, England. Clarkson had worked on the conservation of many ancient and medieval manuscripts, including such treasures as the *Samaritan Pentateuch*, a 13th-century codex, and Hereford Cathedral's *Mappa Mundi*.

Above: Lifting off a 1948 parchment strip.
Above, right: Dissolving glue remaining from the 1820 binding.

Initial Assessment

Clarkson's first task as he disbound the Bible was to produce a detailed conservation report, both written and photographic. An area of special interest was whatever lay hidden in the binding. In 1820 the Bible was rebound in three volumes by Charles Lewis, one of the most fashionable binders in the West End of London; so fashionable indeed that he took to wearing Hessian boots with tassels. There was a fear that, in the manner of his time, Lewis had used hot rabbit skin glue on the spine-folds. Being collagen like the parchment, this adhesive would attach itself to the parchment and even dissolve it where there was contact, namely at the outer spine-fold of each quire.

The fear proved justified. Worse than that: when in 1948 Miss Beatrice Forder attempted to remove the dry glue deposits, she 'skinned' the parchment surface, as well as causing holes and tears along the spine-fold. Most of these she repaired with full-length strips of sheepskin parchment, unfortunately applied with paste and too wet. On drying they contracted, causing cockling across the outer sheets of each quire. All these strips had to be removed, along with the vestiges of 19th-century glue, to leave the spine-fold clean, if vulnerable.

Dry Cleaning

The first major task Clarkson undertook was to remove accumulated dirt and grime, especially from the most displayed surfaces. The results for this were surprisingly good, though the bottom margin of the leaf was harder to clean because the oils from people handling the manuscript there had fixed dirt into the open weave of the belly flank of the calf.

The dry cleaning was an extremely exacting process that involved lifting off the dirt with a variety of different soft-hair and fine-bristle brushes and erasers of differing density. To avoid a lighter border being created around an untreated block of text, leaving a halo effect, Clarkson had to rub around the contours of the letters themselves, mainly under magnification. Dry cleaning just one page could take several days.

Dry cleaning with an electric eraser.

Repairing and Stabilising

Each outer two-leaf spread (bifolium) was gently humidified in a cabinet and then pinned out with clips onto a board to ease the remaining stiffness in the spine. Clarkson then repaired the spine-folds with parchment patches cut to fit the exact space of the gap and not leave a ridge around the edges. Patching was a technique known to the monks; indeed, there are some original scriptorium patches in the Bible that repaired imperfections in the calfskin.

Where illuminated letters had been cut out, leaving large holes in the leaf, patching

was not the preferred solution. The experts group decided that the best way to increase the structural support for these leaves was, where necessary, to reinforce the gap with strips of parchment. These had to be cut so as not to obscure any of the text around the edge of the hole. Fortunately, this was not a common problem.

Some of the illuminated letters needed considerable attention. Over the years of display light had not only irreversibly faded some of the colours, but also attacked the pigment binder, loosening the colour particles and making them friable. The binders in the foundation for the gold leaf had also been affected in places, causing portions to loosen and even flake away in plates from the parchment surface. The solution to both these problems was to use various consolidants. Clarkson took great care to ensure that the right dilution and quantity of these were used to avoid the repaired areas seeming darker.

Digitising

Once each volume of the Bible had been disbound and their leaves dry-cleaned, repaired and stabilised, the leaves were taken to be digitised. It was possible to lay each pair of leaves quite flat, with negligible distortion toward the spine, and to record the binding marks and everything previously hidden of the editors' marginal notes. These included both the comments of the original scribe in his brownish-black oak-gall ink and later comments of the editor writing in a darker ink containing carbon soot.

Top: Pinning out the parchment to ease stiffness and pleats. *Above:* A tear before and after patching.

Left: Digitising the Bible.
Below: Consolidating the gilding, f.3 St Jerome's letter to Desiderius, *Genesis Initial Master.*

Having the Bible digitised allowed the Cathedral to guard the Bible for the future as much as is humanly possible. Obviously it is impossible to replace a unique historic document, no matter what insurance is paid; but thanks to advances in digital photography it was possible to take images of such detail that they could be reproduced at full scale with no loss of quality. In the event of catastrophic loss an archival copy could at least be printed on vellum to give an accurate representation of the original.

Rebinding

With the digitisation of each volume complete the leaves could be re-formed into quires, ready for rebinding. The experts group pondered over the sort of structure which could best support the manuscript. Fortunately the Romanesque period, when the Bible was written, marked a high point in the design of books. Avoiding all use of glue, it relied on physical means such as sewing, tacking and pegging to allow the leaves to flex and flow naturally, without tension, as the book was opened and closed.

The final design returned to the five stations of the original sewing, rather than the previous seven, and involved sewing in double bands for strength. Another Romanesque feature that was reinstated was having the band-slips laced into the boards via spine-edge tunnels, rather than, as in 1948, by threading through drilled holes from outside the boards.

It was not possible to return to the Romanesque design in every respect. The two volumes of the Bible would have been fully covered with leather. If Bishop Henry had lived to see

Miss Beatrice Forder in the Cathedral Library at Winchester preparing the Winchester Bible for its new covers, 1948.

Beatrice Forder (1901–76) lived with her sister Mildred in a cottage just outside the old city walls of Winchester. She devoted over fifty years to working in the Cathedral Library as an assistant. It was she who sewed back the Obadiah initial after it had been 'found' by Walter Oakeshott in the house belonging to Sir Richard Sykes in Yorkshire and bought back for £400. Beatrice Forder's chief work was to rebind the Bible from three into four volumes in 1948. She based her tooled design for the pigskin quarter-binding on the Exodus Initial (see p.17). When she died the subscription collected in her memory paid for new oak cabinets for the Bible, which were used for the next forty years.

the end of the project his binding would probably have been in tanned leather, ornately tooled; the Cathedral still has a volume from that period, a history of the scattering of the Jews by Hegesippus, bound in this elaborate style. As Henry did not survive, however, the eventual binding may have been more modest.

The experts group decided that for the sake of strength and durability the conventional material for 12th-century monastic binding should be used, alum-tawed calfskin, i.e. skin treated with aluminium salts and softened by an egg fat-liquoring. Although at that time covers could be stained red, green, blue or purple, it was decided that they should be left

cream. And because it is no longer possible to find skins of sufficient quality large enough to cover books of this size, it was also decided to use a quarter-binding, leaving most of the beautifully figured oak board exposed.

The 1948 oak boards were too thin and small to be reused, but like them the new oak boards were quarter-cut, i.e. cut across the width of the trunk to its centre, like a cake, resulting in a characteristic pattern of prominent ray figures. The oak tree selected was one that grew on a slope, causing its centre to move towards the slope and therefore producing the widest possible boards on the far side, from centre to circumference, for this project.

Above, left: The volume of Hegesippus bound and kept in Winchester.
Above: f.203v Book of Obadiah, *Genesis Initial Master over design by Leaping Figures Master* – stitched back by Miss Forder in 1948.

The Future of the Winchester Bible

The conservation of the Bible has opened up a new chapter in research of the Bible. The digital images will allow a worldwide community to examine the entire manuscript, including the instructions of the original scribe previously hidden in the spine-fold. There is also hope that multispectral analysis will shed new light on the composition of the initials and that electron microscopy on the dirt removed from the leaves will reveal something about the conditions in which the Bible was kept before the 1820s when the then Dean had it rebound. The main aim of the conservation, however, has simply been to ensure that generations to come have the privilege and joy of seeing this manuscript in the best possible state.

The Winchester Bible is a treasure that helps us to understand the past, but also it alerts us to our culture's present blind-spots. Type 'Bible' into a search engine and 35 million entries are available in an instant; but wisdom and insight take longer. The painstaking production of the Winchester Bible reminds us that sometimes words are worth lavish time and attention, and that we are not only consumers but those who can be consumed by a passion to seek and find a life-giving message from God.

We live in an age suspicious of religious truth, or indeed of any claims to truth at all, which so often seem oppressive. The Winchester Bible whispers that whatever truth is, it lies very close to beauty; the truth of the Bible is meant to delight both the eye and the heart. St Benedict knew about the eagerness of those who dare to pursue the way of truth, when he ends the Prologue of his Rule with a promise: *As we advance in the religious life and in faith, our hearts expand and we run the way of God's commandments with unspeakable sweetness of love.*

The Winchester Bible remains an open invitation to this life-giving way and a symbol of the beauty of the One who beckons.